C+1

JOELLE TAYLOR is an award-winning poet, playwright and author. A former UK slam champion, she founded SLAMbassadors, the UK's youth slam championships, in 2001 and was its Artistic Director and National Coach until 2018. Taylor is a fellow of the RSA and the host and co-curator of Out-Spoken, the UK's premier poetry and music club, currently resident at the Southbank Centre. Taylor is widely anthologised, and is the author of three poetry collections, three plays and a collection of short stories, *The Night Alphabet* (forthcoming).

www.joelletaylor.co.uk

'Absolutely incredible ... A tribute to the dyke bars and the butches who left their mark, this book reminds the reader that to exist as we do is a form of protest.'
***DIVA Magazine,* Book of the Month**

'A real treat ... in the vivid bar-set poems, Taylor brings a close-knit community to life ... inventive, powerfully moving work.'
The Telegraph ★ ★ ★ ★

'A work of fearsome imaginative and creative reach.'
Fran Lock, *Culture Matters*

'*C+nto & Othered Poems* is unlike anything I've ever read before. Partly autobiographical, it excavates, foregrounds and celebrates the lives of butch lesbians through the most memorable and often astonishing poetry that is at once epic and intimate.'
Bernardine Evaristo's Book of the Year,
Times Literary Supplement

'Joelle Taylor has produced one of the most astonishing and original poetry collections of recent years. [*C+nto*] challenges imprisoning notions of womanhood by celebrating and foregrounding those who face a hostile society when they are only being true to themselves.'
Bernardine Evaristo's Book of the Year,
New Statesman

'*C+nto*, a work that does so much to render the difficult and occluded bodies of butch lesbian women vividly and riotously visible. Throughout the collection Taylor plays a deep concern with the origins, valences and precise meanings of words against the cinematic staging of the poems, producing a conjuration of voice and place that is frankly astonishing.'
Fran Lock's Book of the Year, *The White Review*

'This collection is nothing short of a triumph, weaving emotive and expressive personal histories with a sense of invention in poetic form and structure that should not be overlooked.'
The Idler

C+nto
& Othered Poems

Joelle Taylor

The Westbourne Press

The Westbourne Press
An Imprint of Saqi Books
26 Westbourne Grove, London W2 5RH
www.westbournepress.co.uk
www.saqibooks.com

First published 2021 by The Westbourne Press

3

ISBN 978 1 908906 48 9
EISBN 978 1 908906 49 6

Printed and bound by CPI Mackays, Chatham, ME5 8TD

for my bois, my beautiful bois.

Cunto
— inflection of CUNTARE
(third person singular past historic)

Cuntare
— (transative) (obsolete, literary)
To narrate, tell, or recount (a story)

Contents

the thing I came for:
the wreck and not the story of the wreck

Adrienne Rich, 'Diving into the Wreck'

Preface

This is a book of silences.

C+nto opens in a time of absence. Glass display cases appear across the UK outside the old bars, cruising grounds, and squats that once held the LGBT+ community in parenthesis. They come in the shape of snow globes, fish tanks, jars, crystal music boxes, vivariums, bottles and grand museum cabinets. Each case holds a different scene: first loves, bar fights, arrests, explosions, serpentine Pride marches, an old drag queen, a woman circling a boxing ring, and the old Maryville, a fictious dyke dive bar. This book is a walk through the maze of vitrines, one consistent narrative told in separate parts.

The second chapter looks at personal history and is focused on the loss of my friends, and of my exile as a consequence of my sexuality. It was this second part, from which the collection gets its title, that began this writing journey. Apples & Snakes commissioned me to write an original fifteen-minute spoken word piece reflecting on the word 'protest'. I was on tour in Australia at the time, a distance that gave me the intimacy with the page I needed.

First, they take your mouth. Then the whole of your body. As a young teenager stepping tentatively out of the closet in the early 1980s, I was subjected to constant state-endorsed abuse: spat at in school, punched in the back of the head while walking home, attacked on buses, chased from bars, followed home by whistling men, to name a few. I wear the abuse as a suit.

There is no part of a butch lesbian that is welcome in this world. It was bad when I was a teenager. It is as bad today. While this book is set in what is now thought of as the 'golden age of the gay', we have regressed as a community. Our meeting places, clubs and bars have closed, and we gather in distinct flocks across social media, each flock speaking a different language. We inhabit separate rooms in the same club. If we were to regain the real-life meeting grounds, if we were to be in the same room, then perhaps we would remember our commonality. The internet celebrates difference. The club celebrates unity. In these distinct spaces we learn to protect one another. We learn that we are one another.

O, Maryville follows the narrative of one night in a dyke bar, and is based on an amalgam of some of the dirty oasis I spent my beardless youth in. I wanted to recreate that sense of belonging, especially in terms of an indistinct outer threat. The bar is safe ground and a space for those within to examine their lives. The story revolves around four butch lesbians who observe, nurture and protect the space. Even when the bar is demolished these four women hold their ground. *Dudizile, Angel, Valentine* and *Jack Catch* are composite characters, based on real people I met on the scene.

It is important that we preserve our history. I excavated my own past and that of others through the extensive use of archives, both digital and on location. I interviewed other butch lesbians from that era, and together we began to construct a simple story: exile, friendship, grief, love, courage and threat.

At the time of writing, seventy-two countries criminalise same sex relationships; forty-four explicitly criminalise female homosexuality; eleven jurisdictions support the death penalty for lesbian and gays; and fifteen specifically criminalise trans identities.[1]

Unknown numbers of lesbian and gays have been declared missing in Chechnya during the *Purge*, rounded up by security forces after tipoffs from former friends, neighbours or family. They are transported for interrogation where they are tortured to reveal more names from LGBT communities. Films exist of lesbians being publicly murdered by family members, often at the behest of the police. As males, gay men have more freedom in Chechnya than lesbians, and so some are able to escape the Republic. Meanwhile, lesbians are trapped inside the strict religious state indefinitely, predominantly because of their sex.

Meanwhile, 100 municipalities in Poland have initiated LGBT Free Zones and Pride marchers have been attacked with bottles. In Saudi Arabia, homosexuality is punishable with 100 lashes or death by stoning. In Uganda, the Anti-Homosexuality Act (2014) has led to hundreds of LGBT refugees migrating across East Africa. In parts of South Africa, 'corrective' rape is carried out by gangs of *jackrollers* who search for masculine lesbians. Equally, in Chile, the Red Zone in the mountainous Fifth region is a dangerous area for *la camiona*, who are taken from the streets after nights out or on their way home from work. According to the Human Dignity Trust it is illegal to be a lesbian in almost a quarter of the world's countries.

In the UK, we argue about the correct colours of stripes on a flag while war rages across social media. In

---

1   Statistics taken from the humandignitytrust.org, accessed on 2 January 2021.

the UK, we don't need security forces: we pick each other off. Brexit has led to a nationalist confidence unparalleled since the Second Word War, and bigots from both sides are emboldened to assault homosexual and trans people. The word 'lesbian' is synonymous with that hated epithet, 'TERF', and, as a community, we spend more time policing each other than protecting.

It is against this backdrop of rising global homophobia, transphobia and misogyny that this book is written. I wanted to both acknowledge the crimes against the LGBT community and reflect back to a time when we had a greater sense of unity, of self.

In 2021, we face extreme threats from the outside and division within. Unity has never been more important, but in order to achieve that, we must reflect on our histories, where they converge, where they differ, and make a joint decision on where we are going — and how we get there. We build the road we walk on together.

Everything in this book is preserved: salt, vinegar, alcohol, aspic, in vitrine. Whatever is within remains there.

In case of emergency, break the glass.

— Joelle Taylor
February 2021

Glossary

SCENE POEMS

Scenes — The 'scenes' are visual poems that follow a narrative arc, holding the story together.

LX — Lighting Direction, a shorthand used in theatre scripts to indicate a change in lighting state.

FX — Sound Direction, a shorthand used in theatre scripts to indicate a change in the soundscape. Can be music or ambient sound.

VITRINE

Homunculus — a miniature fully formed human, often depicted in a bottle or jar.

VITRINE REPRISE

royal oak, duke of welly, artful dodger, first out, candy bar the box, due south, the y bar, bliss, the bell, girl bar, fallen angel, WOW, glass bar, AWOL, venus rising, vixens, kitty lips, club kali, bar fusion, substation
  — the names of lesbian clubs, nights or bars that were popular in London during this time period.

Article Three

Actus Reus   — a deliberate physical act of violence that harms another.

Heaven, 1995

The Lighthouse   — London Lighthouse, a centre and hospice for those with HIV or AIDS. It opened in 1986 and closed its building in 2015. The ashes of our gay brothers who died there are preserved in a memorial garden on the old site.

Dudizile *difficult rivers*

Boy-boys   — my own slang for biological men.

Ansisters   — my own slang for female ancestors.

GENERAL NOTES ON SLANG

Butch   — a masculine presenting lesbian

Boi   — a masculine presenting lesbian, often younger

Stud   — a black masculine presenting lesbian

Stone   — a butch who prefers to touch rather than be touched

Femme   — a feminine presenting lesbian

High Femme   — as above, but taken to an extreme

Invert   — medicalised name for a lesbian, circa 1920's

Dyke	— a reclaimed word. Etymology suggests a root in Boudicca and the ceremonial office of the bull slayer.
Bull	— very butch lesbian
Bull dyke	— as above
Bull dagger	— as above
Jack	— old English common slang, as in Gentleman Jack.
Tom	— old English common slang. Also refers to a prostitute.
Diesel	— a working class dyke, often a manual worker, known as *Trade* in LGBT slang
Diesel Dyke	— as above
La Camiona	— Latinx butch
Tribades	— an English term for lesbian, circa 1595
Gold star	— has only had lesbian sex
Silverback	— an elder butch

Vitrine

EXTERIOR: street scene day.

LXI: The sun is a hole in the sky through which the sky is draining.

PULL FOCUS: A man is taking down a sign that reads Old Compton Street & replacing it with a sign that reads Old Compton Street.

ZOOM OUT: Tourists shoal, mobile phones pointing to a series of large glass display cases lining the pavement.

i

& now that Old Compton Street
is a museum & the old bars

are shopping arcades &
the sex cinema a gift

shop & now that
pimps have blue plaques

here come the tourists
dressed as our mothers

circling dead names
cameras triggered

instagramming
our inversion

the small bang.
when my picture is taken

where is it taken to?
who will it become?

Everything, vitrine.
Glass cases line the old roads

materialising beside cruising
grounds & cottages

squats & roughs
fishbowl cenotaphs.

My people, vitrine.
My people, homunculus.

Display cases distinct as dominos
how we all rely on one another

& yet. The cases appear
wherever we once loved.

we display our dead our old
ways our bedroom bunkers

the presence of absence

sunlight handsomes
the cabinets &

the way it is
is the way it was

iii

The glass boxes extend their magic trick

                    Hackney, Vauxhall, Brixton
                    Herne Hill, Clapham,
                    Hampstead Heath,

Canal Street, Kemptown, Hebden Bridge
The Calls, Cathedral Quarter, Churchill Way

                    Hurst Street, The Triangle,
                    Old Market
                    Stanley Street, Merchant
                    City Broughton

Each case   history in parenthesis.

pretty police enter a cottage.
                    a brawl ribbons in still life.
an explosion in aspic.
                    a terrine of a night.
dancers lain across each other.
                    the archaeology of a dance floor.

In this case, reliquary. the bones
of saints & inverts; this femur belonged

to the first boi who over-extended
her stride & that clip of thorax must be

the hive of the lisp, a voice that once held
men to it like *eau d'toilet.* This jawline remembers

winding the words in; maybe the skin knows
something about silence, see how it has turned

from itself. When breath eddies the dust, we are
all born again, my pretty Pompei, settling

into the shape of a street fighter
her petticoats snarling. I am glad

they kept her stare. We fall to our knees,
as we always have, bring the bones

a well-cooked meal. Light gossips the glass
& dust rises like heretic prayer.

Bones belonged
extended the hive.

It remembers.
Knows, turned away.

We are settling.
Street fighter, I am glad

of bones, of glass
of heretic prayer.

vi

in this case

two bois, lawn fresh, bend to kiss
& repeat, their lips lemniscate.

a woman buttons her waistcoat over
a body of sky, & stalls.

Saturday holds its breath & the night leaps
a stylus afraid of what it might say.

history is a man packing a suitcase
what he leaves behind more valuable

than what is taken. What is taken is absence
neatly folded. Only the shirts he will need.

the rest of the house, a chaos.

vii

& here
a boxing ring roped with barbed wire
spotlit in the centre of a glass music box
  clouds of mist rise from a steamer in one corner
  of the ring, where a three-piece suit hangs.
an elder butch sits in the opposite corner on a stool,
head down. She is wearing white boxers and white vest.
  a bell rings.

C+nto

//

some girls fall   from sunlight skies   straight down into
flat-pack floral dresses   grab their smiles   from a hook
behind the door   rescue their faces   from rip tides of
mirrors

some girls are always   falling.

//

ROUND ONE
the body as battleground

you fall   miss your body entirely   land somewhere
in enemy territory   behind the lines   your body   a
foreign country   you cannot get a visa for   your skin
a parachute caught in tree branches   you awaken
in no man's land   gunfire from over the horizon   &
women   are crucified on hashtags across the dark hills.

//

your trench   is crowded with dead women   wearing
faces that try to   escape them   the clothes of someone
you once knew   there are landmines buried deep beneath
your skin   &   no one understands them   *tread softly*
when you walk across me   in between   battle cry &
bedroom   is this   sticky quiet   this   no man's land.

//

men explode when you least expect it.

//

all these lifetimes searching for body.

ROUND TWO
the body as protest

born backward   bright back & wide-skin   rolling
cigarettes & shirt sleeves   skyline chin   Levi's & lips
curled up to cuff   white t-shirt   that they might project
themselves on you   tsunami quiff   a shadow rising
above the dreaming town   & black boots whose roots
spread   tangle   through the centre of the earth.

//

you don't wear make-up   to prove   you have not made
anything up   this is   your face   your father's friends
give it to you   one Christmas eve   1973   you unwrap
it beneath a decorated tree   from which the rest of
your family hang   they sip cocktails   as you disappear
swaying gently to the   wail of celebration   that
harbinger of party.

//

you cut your first suit out of the thick silence when you
enter a room.

//

they call you *butch*   the named derived from Butch
Cassidy   you are the descendant of (out)laws   irony
incarnate   woman butchered   cut into select meats:
middle distance stare   breast   shoulder   wild tongue.
they fear you.

//

boi bwah dyke diesel female sodomite lady faggot bull-dyke
bull-dagger queer pervert gold star silver back stud invert
kiki she-male drag-drone baby butch tomboy stone

//

but if you are a Stone   you are a chip off the mountain
and you join   an avalanche   of wrong-walking women
shaven heads   like tumbling rocks   you keep them close
they are   rosary

//

on the dance floor   we are tidal   heckle the night   we
bat nods between us   handshakes   pull us out of the
currents   landed & breathless.

//

we are untamed   a wilderness of women   we are waste
ground   *what a waste love*   nothing grows on us   sterile
and barren   an un-useful female   empty as church
pews   the wind rattles its fists   inside our wombs   *come*
now, snake boy   *come now*, heretic healer   where are
the maths that solve us? How do we fit into your alge*bra*
your binary code?

//

our bodies are political placards   we dance as
demonstration   of independence   we revolution in
the living room   we uprising in the public toilets
insurgency in the suburbs.

//

fear is a girl backing into her face

//

is it   we are not camp enough to be your best friend
our closet   a strata of fossilised clothes   girl pelt   is it
we are not funny enough   for your talk show   is it that a
woman without make up   is a woman without a face?

//

how were we to know   that when we were cleansing   we
were erasing our whole existence.

//

ROUND THREE
the body as trespass

you are a trespasser in your own body   the landowners
are men   who pass you in the street.

//

& now Accrington city centre cars stammer & words
ejaculate from slit windows   your mother's phone wails
song of insistence   the umbilical cigarette   woman who
taught me to breathe *do you know about your daughter*
& now three Pentecostal pastors   hymning holy Nazi
insignia   break into your home [God is an atheist
who no longer believes in Himself]   they unscrew the
lightbulbs slowly   eyes fixed on the unfinished girl
sobbing war on the corduroy settee & whisper   a prayer
for you to leave your family.

//

& now thirteen   a man pulls you over the back seat of
a bus   and stubs his kiss out on your cheek   slowly   a
boxer's embrace   but he does not throw the punch   he
posts it you wait by letterboxes   flinch when it chatters.
never answer the phone.

//

& now Brixton Town   men cradle their fists like babies
watch as you walk past   as though they are thin ribbed
cats in the undergrowth   & you   a small shaven-
headed bird   there is a reason   that women are likened
to birds   & it has little to do with wings   some songs
harden on the wind   some girls   live in gilded cages
on suburban mantelpieces.

//

& now eighteen   clubbing with the crew   a baby-butch
in the abattoir of beauty   the quiver & frantic   white
girls with bhindis   white boys with dreadlocks   saris &
docs   tribal tattoos   modern primitives   heritage worn
like white flags   like cowardice   & you dance as though
you are stamping out fires   your boots   hammering the
last nails into the coffin of the old gods   strangers hug
& tell each other secrets   you are ecstatic   but then the
light looks away   skinny wolves separate you from the
flock wallpaper   the drugs no longer working   as they
amber-eye you   aberration   &   they must conquer
what they cannot name.

//

& now twenty-three   you finish rehearsals in the
city   with nowhere to sleep   the posh kids wish you
goodnight & you walk   & you walk   & you walk   &

//

he finds you quickly   &   when you come around you
are empty   &   his eyes are full   &   above you   twin
gods   &   he slips into small boy   sleep   thumb slotted
in jukebox mouth   &   this is the first time you think you
are going to be killed   &   when you are not it is
a disappointment   the morning after pill   is
a communion wafer   &   you are forgiven your
trespasses.

//

men   are broken things   breaking things.

//

ROUND FOUR
the body as cemetery

the first time   you die   you drink a bottle of cleaning
fluid   & moths of nurses   wrap you in white swaddling
curses *fuck you*   they whisper   a back alley lullaby
fuck you   they croon   as you are interred in the hospital
bed   when the mourners come   they seem happy
a picnic in a mortuary.

//

the third time   you die   it is classic   cinematic   a
bottle of your mother's sleeping pills   you swallow
without water   watching a film   about a girl who is
not loved   it ends   the cinema empties   but you are
not seen   thin thing   mouth like an earthquake   in
a country no one can spell   they don't find you until
morning   & you are sent away to apologise   to the fat
priests of psychiatry

you lie   and your smile   torn cunnus   a   split.

//

ROUND FIVE
the body as backroom

each night   we have a lock in   & meet at the back of
my heart   smoking in circles   handing grins between
us like pass-the-parcel   opening each layer of the smile
until the pith of it is revealed   we are ferocious women
eating our children   our youth   climbing out of our
skins   & leaving them draped   like soiled wedding
dresses   as we fall into each other's mouths   this is
love   furious love.

//

we die slowly   cigarettes stubbed against obsidian skies
a brain explodes into night butterflies   a car loses its
grip on reality   an understated overdose   suicides by
the bouquetful.

not one of my friends was allowed to live in her body
unaccompanied.

always a lodger   pacing in the box room   always a
landlord   collecting rent.

ROUND SIX
the body as haunted house

in sleep   my body is a haunted house   there are
footsteps along fallopian corridors   the corridor is a
rope strung above a mouth   I have been woken by
blurred voices   without bodies   quiet arguments in my
basement   once I was possessed   by a small girl   who
looked the same as me   who ate herself on a Sunday
afternoon   while her parents   downstairs   hardwired
their hangovers   & Christmas tunes   looped in nooses

//

my heart   is a church bell   but nobody visits   & God
is a man   hands in his pockets   watching.

//

ROUND SEVEN
the body as uprising

o, you bayonet boys   you truncheon rub   my face does
not fit my face   but your fist does   years from now   no
one will remember   how we fought   how each bruised
knuckle   was a white boy's head   bent in prayer   no
one will remember   the love   how alike it is to rage
how screams made corporeal   are rainbows   how
rainbows became corporate logos   how we carved our
epitaphs into a stone wall   no one will remember

//

unpicking acronyms by candlelight.

//

I'll be in the back bar of heaven   Cass will be getting a
round in   releasing that laugh   a flock of wild birds
escaping her mouth   and none of this will matter   I'll
be riding the ghost roads with Valentine   bare back knee
clench on her Harley   I'll be stretching skins with Jack
Catch   or scuffing the city with Dudizile   men will
stare like open shaft mines   I'll be walking   white lines
with Angel   tight mouth   antelope heart.

//

I can't remember   the names   of all my dead friends
but   they are here now   our grief   a leather jacket
our laughter   static   as we   fade to a sepia   the colour
of blood mixed to water   disappearing down a plug hole
much like the meeting   of our legs

//

remember this

//

our whole lives

//

we are.

//

protest.

Vitrine Reprise

viii

& over here the age of unreason
causes without effect, how we circled

our own mute in dim
bedrooms bent over

mirrors looking for the face
within the face looking

for the exit. maybe
you think. maybe. a door

will open in my cheek &
inside will be a room

filled with everyone
I love. we will drink
water. there will be
food.

we will all know
what hands are for.

ix

royal oak duke of welly artful dodger
first out candy bar the box

> due south the y bar bliss the
> bell
> girl bar fallen angel
> WOW glass bar AWOL

venus rising vixens kitty lips
club kali bar fusion substation

x

& here
where the wrong walkers
giddied
a snow globe mounted
on a pedestal

inside, *Maryville*, blinking
all of her wonders, captured.

the wind nailed to the wall.

O, Maryville

SCENE ONE

EXTERIOR night. A main road in London.

LX1: Streetlamps watch a woman pass & text each other.

FX1: The sound of a door opening into a chest cavity. A
lone woman walks briskly, head down & holding invisible
bouquets. Ahead of her is a hunched building with its
hands in it pockets, bracketed by gossiping fairy lights.

LX2: A neon sign flashes its pink dilate. *Maryville*, the
sign says. The woman pushes open the door & enters
her own body. At the bar she orders a drink and when it
arrives it is her breath. Music is playing. It is the sound
of someone being listened to. She notices that she is
sitting at every table. When the woman asks her to dance
the whole of her past stands up to dance with her; her
classmates, her teachers, the manager of the shop she
worked in over Christmas, the newspaper proprietor, the
street she grew up on, an adjacent town, her parents and
grandparents, the kid who waited for her after school.
The song ends. The world opens. Venus rises.

Psalm

o Maryville / song of loose shirt / you button down boi
/ you thick rod of irony / o, Maryville / you sawn-off
mini skirt / you tights torn into choir / o Maryville/ o
swagger / o keychain & denim / i am plural / o Maryville
/ we dress as our greatest fears / we dress as ourselves
/ o Maryville / the etymology of dyke / so many holes
to fill / i knew your mother / saw them / lower her body
/ into her body / saw how she became cenotaph / the
neighbourhood children left flowers at / o Maryville / i
remember your sister / how antelope she was / how she
froze when she heard the first roar / how she fell into the
o of the roar / o Maryville / the antelopes are eating the
antelopes / o my Maryville / forgive us / their trespasses.

o, Maryville / let us walk alone at night / & let the night
not follow us / let us drink too much / & awaken in
each other's mouths / o Maryville / let us be ugly / let
us unwash / let us language / our mouths are filled with
men / line dancing / let us pass the half smoked cigarette
/ o Maryville / let us fatten / let us leave our faces /
on the back seat of night buses / let someone take a
photograph not of us / but because of us / let our limbs
grow wild / our hair retreat / our hormonal seas / let
our breasts // let them // let us inherit each other's teeth
/ o Maryville / keep us alive this death / keep us from
prayer / deliver us from ego / for thine are the body / the
birthing & the burning / forever & ever // *are you a man*?

A Lesbian Walks into a Bar

o holy church of
Maryville on our knees
by Sunday looking up
our own skirts the tables
are a strange atoll
each with its own
customs but we share
a root language a lesbian
walks into a bar or
a bar walks into a
lesbian how it is to
arrive what it is to
become o holy i stand
at the bar side knowing
when i look up i will be
serving myself & when i
am done that i will take
the drinks to a table
where i am waiting
& later on, i'll
give glad eye
to a girl & she
will be me.

SCENE TWO

INTERIOR, Maryville. Night.

LX1: the orange of belief.

FX1: the sound belonging makes. Three elder butches
& a younger boi share a table. Maryville knows them
all by name, pulls them to her breast: *Dudizile, Angel,
Jack Catch & Valentine.* They conference the night. The
evening swirls around them as though they are stones
in a river. Sometimes, other bois rest with them. Mostly,
they are architecture. The four friends know this room.
The four friends are this room.

LX2: light narrows to a cartoon spotlight.

Valentine

Born right body
wrong day, Valentine
flicks her lighter
in the corner of the club
& white women flutter.
Tonight, she has dressed
as the inside of a mouth
a handsewn suit excised
from a cured night sky
black leather has its own skin
care routine it listens
to its mother i have heard
it said some girls give birth
to themselves on the back
of motorbikes invent the wind
let the road uncurl from between
their legs, the infinite motorway
something British & unbidden
i know why we are drawn
to the corners it's where the road
cannot reach us. Every part
of a woman is a weapon
if you know how to hold her
Valentine says. The corner
flicks a Morse & in the dark
white hearts beat like moths
against a headlight.

Angel

When Angel looks in the mirror / it looks away first /
star fist open jaw / how the shine becomes you / clean
friend / taller than yesterday / spine an unravelling plot /
you odd insistence / my king of the blue tattoo / eyebrow
pinned like a butterfly / when you walked in the room
/ it became you. How you brought the silence in with
you. How you brought the night to its knees. back there.
where the quiet ones go. / & now / the night won't stop
texting / how many times have we walked home / you &
I / only to find home walking / softly behind us / I have
seen you leap over language / to push a man back inside
himself / throw pint glasses like seeds / speak to every
woman as though she were your mother / I have seen
your fists sob / at the centre of every boi / is a bare room
/ & inside a swinging lightbulb / a wire thin girl dances
/ stays with you even when you look away / angels don't
fall from Heaven / they leave at closing time / unscrew
their fucks in the backs of black cabs / abandon their
bodies / beneath a girl beneath a duvet beneath the wet
dilated night. on fire.

Dudizile

Dudizile steps out
of the closet
straight into a
mahogany tallboy
brokered from Islington
market strung with raw
slabs of bright
suits Donegal herring
bone the way of things
double helix weave
houndstooth Harris
how we were
beside each suit
hangs a boy she
once loved a blue
twill cadet
a well-spoken rent boy
the pelt of a father
turning. Vintage
Givenchy haunts
the tie rack &
white shirts wait
quiet & replete
only wanting the
best for her.

Jack Catch

my boi / water carved stone / something the sea placed
on the end of your bed / has been in the corner of the
bar / for so long the locals pray / beneath her / leave
garlands of violets / wrapped around nautical crosses /
they say she was a sailor / caught perfumed fish with her
bare hands / her heart a compass / *a boi is not a boy but
a buoy*[2] / they say / she renovated airplane engines / that
she understood air / what it wants / or that she was oil
/ something hard worked / brought up from the core /
that powers everything else / the fairy lights flutter their
belief / when she walks past / more comfortable / in their
illusion / the wallpaper / wants to undress / & the ribald
carpet / soft as any onenight / has learned the beauty of
submission.

---

2   life buoy

SCENE THREE

DOWNSTAGE left, a woman in matching skirt and blazer rushes onto the stage from the audience & anxiously hauls open a door marked *Maryville*.

INTERIOR: Maryville

LX1: the orange of hello.

FX1: low swung jazz, the sound of voices collapsing in conversation. The woman, head to chest, walks briskly though the bar to the toilets.

INTERIOR: toilets.

LX2: the strip light flurries its eyes at her. The woman enters the toilet and locks the door.

FX2: the sound of air unzipping, the world peeled; the music of a woman giving birth to herself. The cubicle door opens, & a butch casually steps out, in tweed trousers, button shirt and blazer. At the sink she drowns her hair and places the dead pet on her head. She opens the bar door like a second date.

FX3: loud swing music, mouths are amphitheatres. At the end of the evening a skirt parachutes her to safety.

Article Three

Between 1940s and 1960s, US police arrested lesbians wearing less than three pieces of traditional women's clothing. They were often publicly stripped.

when they search her   they are looking for her body
where she buried it   is it beneath your bed they say   do
the floorboards know you   can you remember the field
if the sun   was like this   &   the tree   was like that
where are you   your mother   reported you missing:
she said   the echoing bed   a rind of skirt & blouse   I
kissed her good night   your mother said   & in the
morning   a strange man   was in her bed   his hands
red   his eyes chattering doorways   so we chased him
away from everything   that made us. Your mother said
she lit a candle in the window   does the light attract
the dark?   they found your clothes   but not your body
actus reus   did you snort the chalk outline   is your true
flag   red   then blue   then red?   i did not see me   the
woman said   that night or any other   but dogs   braille
the ground   the air holds voices.

//

when they search her   their hands are   the first men
to enter the village   guns cocked   some wild reckoning
doing it for the kids   they are   looking for where   the
rebels are hiding   the enclave   the poem returning to
the hand   a tight-lipped press   radio humming the wall
they are looking for   the girl who   hides   all the girls
the one   who turned the rainbow into a railway track
but the villagers   keep building more houses to search

& the woman is always one street ahead   her heels tap
a telegram   answered by outlaws & when they arrive
it is in the nick of time   an ankle disappearing into a
helicopter   that's the problem with women like this
they say   as soon as you find her   she is gone   it's like
holding   a hole.

//

when they search her   they are showing her   her own
body   this is your breast   they powerpoint   a projector
opens its damp eye   the breast goes here   like this   &
I   like this   & you   spine a ladder of water   (we are
all of us water drowning)   the last part of her   body
they show her   is her tongue   the police & the woman
crowd   around the   /o/pen palm   of the sergeant
gazing down at the thing   its pink grief   the sergeant
dreams   i remember   he says   when the canals
galloped thick with these   & shoals of tongues   fought
their way upstream   to rumour the river   & you could
just   stand in the water   grey as a road   & pull them
out   with your   cupped hands.

//

SCENE FOUR

INTERIOR night. The bathroom of the Maryville bar.

FX1: Music with a hand over its mouth.

FX2: Voices clamber over each other.

LX1: A fluorescent strip light undresses & the white tiles watch. The set is dressed in three toilet cubicles, three sinks, one long mirror over the wash basins, and an out of order hand dryer. Toilet tissue calligraphies the tiles. The cubicle doors open simultaneously and three suited bois walk out. They stand at the sinks letting the taps talk while their eyes find each other in the mirror. It is always this way. They say nothing but there is a nod, small as a first word. The boi in the centre finishes washing her hands, shakes them dry, then carefully reaches toward the butch, stage left. The tie, she says, and gently straightens it.

Homosapien

Song by the Buzzcocks, a punk gay anthem.

//

i am a shy boi. you are a coy boi.

//

angerland / deep north / the year of the zip / I was
a girl who had grabbed her body / from the wrong coat
hook / laughter followed like a skinny dog / one I learned
to tame / with hands that knew my father / I threw my
childhood / & the dog brought it back / Thursday night
/ the school disco erupts into nothing / boys shuffle their
faces / & girls pick one / curl an edge / I cut my profile /
from a pattern in NME / but the seams still show / white
lines in the school disco.

//

bad girls gather like cigarette smoke / their night talk /
swarming / above the heads of binary dancers / the lit
ends of their cigarettes / winking / tinker taylor hello
sailor / an insolence of leather jackets / the warm outrage
of indifference / kiss me until my mouth opens into
a career / darling, you / bad grammar grin / shark fin
Mohican / swim across the dance floor to me / tinker
taylor hello sailor / my gender / is exile.

//

my tongue jumps / a needle with a penny sellotaped
on top / & you steady me / with a look in a different
language / & my heart an uprising / so when you say
/ that Kevin got sent down / for that brief holiday at
the cottage / we know each other / have inherited the
same tradition of longing / a language of full stops / we
speak most clearly / when we are not speaking / how
bad girls / have always found each other / bin detritus /
underage thinker / wrong walking woman / you must be
homosapien too.

//

we say nothing   walk like enemies
                    into the single bed of a rough brick wall

the Unbelong

    (i)   daughter

we are all born grieving   that is why babies cry.

i am birthed   walking backward into the wind
apologising   making peace treaties   with my skin. see a
small girl   haunt a television   see a small girl tap dance
across knuckles.

strangers take their faces off when I enter rooms. I am
unborn   sing the Unbelong   swim against the tide of
tongues   I am the girl with the face of a man   crack
thin   cold as school corridors   I am tangled cotton
speaking in knots.

but I have two hands   each of them dog. I teach them
to fetch   to hunt   retrieve   they sleep curled at the
bottom of my bed   my dogs   strain at their leash   bite
children. when I open my mouth   a bugle led hunt
streams out.

violence is its own mother. mother breast feeds fists.
violence is a girl backed up against herself   everything
about her   ghost   everything   bed.

when I leave home, it follows me.

(ii)   mother

the past is always slightly ahead   peering around a red
brick corner   warming the wet bed   smoking a cigarette.

i rent a separate flat for my body to live in   while I
write myself into the world   feeding thin slithers of raw
promises   to the empty mouths of purses   watching
flocks of pockets   disappearing over the skyline

there are girls who have nothing to eat but themselves
their small spines flagpoles   stuck into soft mattresses in
Brixton bedsits   all of our mothers are warnings.

in the morning   I dress in the reflection   of the class
ceiling   careful colours   the shade of the Unbelong   I
am my mother in my father's suit   still the girl with the
face of a man   still wrong walking.

(iii)   Sister

my sisters   who taught me   to throw punches like life
rings   into bad water   my sisters   bowling hearts
red hand grenade

my sister   bomb shelter   my sisters giving birth to
battlefields   my sister a battlefield

my sisters excavating chests   thick sediments of silence
ovarian necklaces   my sisters archaeologists

my sisters   unclipping their shadows   and setting them
free   my sisters   whose graves give birth   my sisters
who store their smiles between their legs

my sisters   who tamed my fists   had them vaccinated
spayed   my sisters   who stroked my face   back into its
kennel

my sisters   who taught me to   pluck the weeds   from
my tongue   pull the pin out of a poem   & cover my
ears

my sisters   listen   can you hear?

           outside   dogs have begun to bark their real
           names   & no longer   flinch   when kissed

my sisters   watch   can you see?

           a small girl walks into her body
                       & turns the bedroom light on.

Angel — the destroyer

Angel / working out the riddle of her body / bench press
the sky / curl the weight of hope / angels strip search
themselves / shower in grown men's tears / dress in full
camouflage / not shemale / but an antelope stalking
alongside the lions / when she pulls on her boots / she
is pulling someone out of water / when she leaves the
flat / she is the first foot in an impossible place / her
flag / a picture of herself / with her back turned / brute
mother / loving rage / she plucks the rainbow out of its
wound / flicks it into a whip / some girls carry the storm
in their mouths / some in their palms / she named her
third knuckle after you / so it would always remember /
its birth language / & tonight / Matthew / she will make
friends / from the offcut of enemies.

Valentine — creation myth

it is said she
built her motorcycle
from spare washing
machine parts an
old Nintendo controller
& a flick knife
her brother left
her but when
the doors close
Valentine opens
she told me
that the bike
grew from her
that her arms
chromed into handlebars
while she slept
that she dreamed
she gave birth
to the road
that it took
a long time
but her toes
clenched into wheels
scapular fuel tank
eyes signalling left
her back folded
to carry us all
home & she
learned how to
lean into fear.

Dudizile — everything in its place

in the third
drawer of a
rusting filing cabinet
sit the folded the
ready the clean
all white rows
arms crossed sit
up straight the
boxer shorts the
socks the vests
filed neatly beside
the curled tongues
of ties at rest.
Dudizile can map
read, knows the
way out of her body
is not the
way out her body
when she tightens
her tie in the mirror
she sees herself
standing behind
it's a magic trick
the reflection returning
to the face.

SCENE FIVE

UPSTAGE centre: a revolving mirror ball pedestal.

LX1: spotlight on pedestal.

FX1: the silence of people waiting to speak. The pedestal is dressed in a giant pint of lager. A Busby Berkeley of bois, tuxedoed & monochromatic, synchronise swim in it. From above they make the shape of a three ringed kaleidoscope which dilates to make the shape of a flower exiling seeds, which ejaculates into the shape of a star system unravelling its knowing, through which they make the shape of DNA understanding itself, which opens to make the shape of a virus in a petri dish, which turns to look at you, then unlocks to make the shape of rows of hushed beds that link arms and become a protest across a bridge, that they also make, then a line of butches giving blood, a lesbian abseiling into Parliament, the shape of silence, & as grand finale, collapse into the News at Ten. It's all about the timing.

FX2: rapturous applause.

Heaven, 1995

vinegar this moment of belief.
club in a fish tank, riot genesis
a boi touches her fingertip
to a light beam & god winks
a wet eye. maybe the light
is an escalator to the afterlife,
or after party, or the part of her body
she checked in the cloakroom,
but tonight, all of the dead
will dance with her.
all of the dead are well
dressed this evening.
they solemn the escalator
descend to the dance.
tequila mockingbird releases
her wig back into the wild
blows a kiss that exhales
into carrion birds
the caw of bad lipstick
numb beaks scattering
round white seeds
from which Gaultier
sailors grow, haloed
in certainty, their muscles
the shaven heads of women
marching back into their bones
a clearing at the centre
of them. the butches
peel off their shirts
& underneath
they are children.

salt this boi.
how she reaches
toward the infinite.
this moment between.
how she sees
the ghosts of those
still alive.
how she conjures
life from life.
how The Lighthouse
winks at the storm.

Jack Catch — *teaches at the old school*

jack catch / in her houndstooth suit / oxblood brogues
/ knitted tie / sharpens the air she walks through / the
room sucks its stomach in / tries not to look / she can
undo a bar with one hand / old school / preserved in
the amber of lager / Maryville is aspic / fixing all the
silverbacks / at 7.32pm 1995 / hair you could picnic
on / bring the family / aftershave is a happy man / the
music has been remembering its childhood / scratching
its hazy outline for hours / when Soho & her girls / the
side streets slung / around their necks as feather boas
/ slide in on silk / each wearing her mother pinned to
her breast / pearls low hanging fruit / & the old bois
stop talking / each afraid of her own face / that it might
eat her / but Jack Catch / stands / pulls a chair out of
her sleeve / tips the bar man / taps a cigarette / to stand
out from the others / & when Soho asks for a light /
she is speaking of forgiveness / & when Jack opens
her zippo / she is showing how easy it is to burn / how
aspic dissolves / & now the silverbacks / look toward
saloon doors that never open / young things eddy &
glamour / are paintings of themselves / & old Jack Catch
/ straightens the crease in her houndstooth / says / *jesus* /
are all women female impersonators / says / everything
is running back inside / there are new words for words /
& surveying the club / mutters / I remember

when all of this was / a loose stone / in a wall.

Fist Fucking in the Yemen

one man knocks at the door but five push their way in
ransack the living room kindly their pockets plump with
misgiving pull out a string of coded handkerchiefs pull
a woman from a rabbit a puppet show erupts inside a
boi & suddenly jazz (you & me boyband, baby) *I fell
in love with the way men die* we have been here before
a small child has fallen down a hole & a dog comes to
shout about it so you go in crawl belly white note the
shadow of your father mottling the wall the job is too
big, so you call for help & it helicopters in it launches in
it tanks on in & afterward you write a song about it. *I like
my women bored and neurotic.* when you sleep, you dream
of men standing still. there is a lock & the lock is also the
key & what you need to do is turn yourself.

SCENE SIX

INTERIOR living room Hackney, evening.

LX1: lamps consider their fingernails. A young boi, head shaved into topiary, holds a pair of cheap clippers.

FX1: the belly of the clippers' growls.

FX2: a tape cassette player fingers ribbon like rosary as Trade Volume One paces the room. Other bois gather around a chair at which a young stud sits, Red Stripe can in hand. She has her hair tied up in dreadlocks, and the younger white boi is worrying. Peter, she laughs, just fucking do it. Peter does. The hair falls like binary code and where it lands a forest grows and the forest is full of wild and the wild is full of apology and the apology is full of tiger and one of them jumps up at the stud in the chair and eats her, head-first. It is all so sudden. No one moves, even as she is devoured. Afterward they all continue to stare at the chair. The white boi stays there for nine years. George, she says. George.

Summer All Night Long

bois, soft skinned & shaven,
shelter from the sun in the shadows
cast by elder butches, kick balls
& catch each other
sketch out a cunnus
with billiards & recreate
the moment of conception.
There are only so many holes
a boi can fall down
but here she is again
& maybe the film reel jumps
a little here, by which I mean heart,
& when I say heart
what I mean is film.
bois are newly planted
as she passes, (there is a reason
storms are named after women)
feel their roots reach out
to each other, bend into her
yes, and one boi,
her tongue a diving board,
launches into her fathom.
nothing as concrete
as a back clap.
nothing as young
as slapped palms.
but still the bar knows
what it knows
that a tongue is a bed
& this
boi understands

how to make it,
origami the sheets
into something
wild and confident
a swan or the hadron
collider, & they will practice
their careful all night.
morning will leave
by the backdoor, never call.
but the boi dreams.
thinks, maybe this time
something will be born.
thinks, if I had a baby,
I would call it
Flinch.

//

the music is big boned, takes up
the whole of the dance floor, is
its own god. light has poor
impulse control, throws herself
at the feet of willow bois
while summer waits
by the open door, fans herself
as bois beg water, reminds us
that bois are almost all water
in the act of becoming
all the bois swept out
the bar on flash tides
of their own belonging.
the music is on
its knees, heavy breathing

across some girl
the weight of unison
almost too much
to bear, but the track
is bullied
back by another
& as the song
climbs to its feet
we throw our hands in the air
& when they land
they are someone
else's.

//

two truths can exist in the same space.
they lean at opposite ends of the bar
turned away from one another
watching the others reflection
in her pint.
her architecture.
her present. her unyielding.
we are caught in the space
between magnetic poles.
these old enemies
shouldering the roof
the whole damn sky
if one moves
the other dies.
these stones in the river.
these deciders of the
tide.

//

it might be tuesday   thursday   doesn't matter
Maryville is waiting   a woman walks into a bar   &
nothing happens   her drink arrives on time   and is
the taste of a drink   her friends materialise beside her
the bar boi   asks if she is going on to the club   & for a
moment   it's ok   everyone in the bar is everyone she
knows. when the night ends   it doesn't.

//

SCENE SEVEN

INTERIOR day time.

LX1: the day does not have her make up on. A bland sun saunters through municipal stained-glass windows.

FX: a pre-recorded hymn on a tape. Jesus is rising but no one looks up.

EXTERIOR daytime. A coach arrives in a car park. Sign: *Birmingham Crematorium.* The coach doors open and a river of butches, bois, studs, femmes, dykes, queens & queers waterfall to the unhappy tarmac. A bird sings something but no one joins in.

INTERIOR: the crematorium. The waterfall fills most of the seats, and laps into the aisles, flooding the shoes of family members.

LX2: nothing.

Angel — heel boi

Angel keeps her fists tied up / with thread to the end
of the bed post / found them mewling / at the side of
the road / ribbed & diseased / now feeds them a diet
of social media / a saucer of lager / takes them for a
nocturne around the estate / letting them sniff the
lampposts / the edges of things / what was meant / if she
leaves them unattended / they howl their glad remorse /
making promises to the windows / & when they sleep / if
they ever do / they dream of a time / when fists were free
/ & fruited every family tree.

Valentine — snow globe

& then there was the time
Valentine squatted a snow
globe, used a communal crow
bar to prise open its legs
& shifted herself & every friend
from the club that night
into it. by morning we had blankets
as curtains & sleet fainted like silk
nightgowns across the beds
dark circuses Wurlitzed
our eyes & we shared
a mirror full of starting lines
knowing that at any moment
we were going to begin.
but the floor kept falling
to the sky. but we kept forgetting
our lines. In the living room
snow dropped like dot to dot
connect them to make a family
names tore free of their moorings
& we were all coloured
outside the lines, all
blizzard. I'll be mother
Valentine growls
her mouth an exhaust
pipe we press our lips
to.

Dudizile — difficult rivers

she speaks difficult
rivers knowing too
many bois are lost
in them those rip
tides of sudden belief
the undercurrent of
language she speaks
dangerous dance
the eros of survival
too close together
in here on a weeknight
she speaks hands untouch
head decline. Dudz only
looks at you from the side
aware of the drift
of boy-boys washing up
in the corners of bars
across the city
sits downwind
grazing with an avalanche
of elder bulls or conducting
a choir of whistling dogs
keeps her tie straight
as tongues something red
for a girl to walk up.

Jack Catch — to the lighthouse

i

we have saved / each other's lives so many times / she
says to the bois / we have become lighthouses / sweeping
the dark gossiping seas / the crowded head bobbing
under / all our girls / adrift on the dance floor / we have
pulled each other / out of the wreckage of our own
bodies / sat beside each other / straight backed / making
islands of each other's bruises / promising that one day
/ we would live there / remember that time / that Angel
intervened / in a street row between real boys & girls / &
we were picking insults / out of her for days / she says /
or that time I was followed / out the bar / remember –

ii

— all of the corner boys / stripped to their white vests
/ muscles a difficult terrain / off the road / skin, a
saxophone / the sweat making sequins / & Jack knows
/ this isn't about beating her / their mannish pinata /
it's a slow dance with each other / someone once said
/ violence is the only way / men can touch / if so / she
is glad to have introduced them. she opens her arms &
they climb in. there are red rose petals.

SCENE EIGHT

INTERIOR, MARYVILLE. Night.

LXI: Sweat rises from the dance floor & knits a rainbow.
It arches above heads, bridging the room. The rainbow is
a spectrum, & we are lined up in order of truth.

FX1: The sound of arrival. All the bois are here, butches,
femmes, the leather dykes, the scene queens, the hand-
reared on lipstick, the frantically ordinary & we dance
together like virus. The contagion spreads until the bar
is a petri dish, club through a microscope, hands raised
as if deflecting God, shouting *Frankie Knuckles*, sweating
I need your love. It is as the frenzy of secular worship
peaks that Angel bursts though the door. Her face is not
her face. The piercing in her eyebrow has been torn out
& blood migrates, looking for a better life. Inside the
wound is a young girl rocking.

FX2: Outside, men are menagerie, their howls tearing
strips of black off the night sky. The evening is in
ribbons. Beneath the black is a white tiled room.

A Woman Steps Out of Her Wound

one hole in the centre of a boi   & the whole town   falls
in behind her   her parents sucked in feet first   still
clutching the semi-detached tablecloth   the bathroom
mirror   her face still sticking to it   then her elder
brother is pulled in too   & he grabs   the hand of his
girlfriend   & she also is absorbed   & her parents; the
whole of the boi's class in school   plummet to the
centre of the wound   dragging her first day at the local
college behind them   & all succumb to the gravitational
force of the wound the   black hole at the centre of a boi.

//

the wound is a circus ring   & the circus brings the town
to it   see how the animals animal   see how the girl   is
almost a girl   see the bois grow out from their wounds
head first   when the trapeze artist loses   her grip on
the narrative   the townsfolk watch silently   as she
tumbles to a dust   that they draw a Venn diagram   of
a wound & an exit in   when the ambulance comes   it
flashes a bright blue gash   & its gaudy o   is a pinhole
in a door   *you can see the future through the hole in a girl*
the doctor   says   & the boi leans over   sees herself
step out from the wound   whose edges applaud in red
velvet   grief   sees herself   wear her wound as a cape, as
a caul   that she raises as one of her own   dresses in
schoolboy suits   *well well well*   the doctor smiles   it
must be true   what does not kill you   makes you
make you.

SCENE NINE

//

INTERIOR day time, crematorium.

LXI: spotlight on a coffin raised on a white wood dais.
The coffin's mouth is open in surprise.

FX1: hymn of shuffling feet. Psalm of awkward. People
line up along the centre aisle. We follow a young white
boi as she moves closer to the box. She is startled to
find not her friend the stud inside, but a young woman
in a cerise ballroom dress, as though the coffin were the
display case for a doll. Her face is battered with makeup.
Her hair is hair but the boi knows that under the wig
the stud has a clean undercut. Her severed strings are
arranged carefully around her. The woman in the coffin
looks at the woman standing over her. The woman in the
coffin looks like a woman.

//

Angel — in the red corner

bare knuckle fighting is a kind of birth / blood o / hands
newly born / Angel stands in the centre of her own ring
/ paws persuaded into doormen / violence / its own grief
/ palms raised in almost prayer / a woman / pacing the
square of her / blood cells / do women fight like we are
climbing out of holes / & what shall we name this night
/ & how shall we guide it / & what will it become / this
wide need / once it has left the fist / how will it learn / to
walk to sing?

Legend of the First Butch

there is a story / the elders used to tell / gathered in
circuses / long into the low breathing evening / listen
daughters / this is / the legend of the first butch / hushup
/ let's say her name was Mary / & let's say she grew
wrong / limbs pulling away from the sun / let's say she
didn't fit her own body / too tight around the seams /
let's say / she kept touching her face / well / one day /
Mary sewed her skirt up the centre / fastened the top
button of her bouse / rolled up each sleeve / licked her
hair down / with Vaseline / & walked down the road like
she was alive / she sat by herself in a bar / & nobody
called the police / she travelled at night / & young men
nodded to her / she was a deer holding a rifle / a cow
milking her master / but the price of freedom / is the
knowledge you are trapped / & she found it more and
more difficult / to be anyone but herself / & on her night
strolls / she recognised other women like herself / the
way their eyes ricocheted off her / & thought to herself
/ what if / there were a place for us / some country / a
land in parenthesis / it is fact / she said / that if you dig
a water hole / all the animals will come / but if you put a
pink light in the window / the lions will think it is they /
who are bleeding.

Dudizile — the first stone

tweed understands the idea
of her, knows where to press
who to call, how to thread a sheep
through a lion, remembers
how like a field
it is, how like freedom & the
waistcoat knows when it needs
to clench, her jacket an elder butch's
arm across her shoulders, thinks
is the only way out of woman
man? How can the exit
also be the fire?
Dudizile does not
get dressed, she unlearns
drapes her ansisters
around her, is wearing
a suit of ghosts tonight
look how she shines
how they stand
beside her & speak
through her

they say: be careful
my mannish daughter
walk backward.
the first stone

is returning.

Angel — young bull

when the boy-boys surround her / she notices their / o /
& gives them both her cheeks / the young bull / kneeling
/ the steam that rises might be spirits / might be release
/ the best way for her to fight this night / is to not fight
at all / allowing their hands / to understand themselves
/ comprehend their works / their blood architecture /
all the sanguinary cities they have built / at the side of
streets / these roadside reformers / these cleaners / their
fists play together in the park / & tonight children / they
are teaching / a woman *how to* / & she takes each punch
/ into her / gestates it / knowing / one day she will give
birth to / a herd of wild hands.

Got a Light, Jack?

I am wondering / if / after I walk into the light / I will
be met by myself / that dead part of me / or whether
it will be the dog / who loved me / whose name I can't
remember / I was once bitten / by a woman / so hard that
I / popped out of my skin like / I want to say mango /
as they are poem fruit / but it was more like / that time /
Angel went in without thinking one Sunday afternoon /
after the afterward / and the fictional condom split / this
is a gay bar / not the Caribbean / though we are certainly
/ birds of paradox / & the broken cistern / might be a
waterfall / & the elocution of women fucking / might be
something edging / closer to the beach / with tide in its
teeth / I never open my mouth when I smile / I don't
want to fall out / an empty bed swings in my chest / is
death like running on to the pitch? / will I be there /
in the centre of the field / arms open like club doors /
asking me to love me?

SCENE TEN

INTERIOR, MARYVILLE. Night.

LXI: the spotlights have become search lights. The dance floor stands back against the wall, listening to

FXI: the world being re-written. What was alive is now sickly, what was proud is now wondering at her clothes. No one believes herself.

Maryville, tender. Maryville, soft. Valentine and Jack walk across the bar, order a pint and lay it Angel's feet. They take her in their arms. The door bulges leaving the imprints of lost men in the wood.

FX2: the sound of circling.

The Battle of Maryville

//

Valentine

the men outside
are men outside.
Valentine wonders
if it is always
the same men outside
if they   want
the same thing.
they want to come
in   the locked room.
the occupied body.
she muses   it is the long road
back to a mother, the baby
who turns at birth, who knocks.
there is a crack in the display
case's idea of itself   outside
naked knuckles shiver together
their towels half-slung around waists
or flicking like tongues
at the backs of legs.
Valentine understands
that to some boys
no is an act of aggression.
voices are thrown   but miss.
the first bottle that spins
into the bar   lands
with its neck pointing
toward her   the bar dilates

& we are film noir.
Valentine cracks open a grin
picks up the bottle   considers
glass: atoms coming together
in short order   inside the bottle
is a bar   its lights blinking
bewilderment its tiny women
gazing up at her. when the
bottle breaks the world pours
out & the flood rises
from our swivel backs
arms link like chromosomes
& Maryville is nation
facing the door that leads
to every door & what is a door
but the only way home.

//

Angel

what circus, what zoo.
Dudz wonders how war
can be civil, while Jack
contemplates the quantum
physics of fighting
if on a molecular level
every woman here is
inside the ring of her
blood cell waiting
for the bell, but Angel
o Angel, her white
fire kindling, walks forward

knowing her fear is
a dress she can no longer
fit into. Around her
the bar convulses. Angel
knows when fists fly
they do not return
not even for seeds
on windowsills.
she holds her whole
self against the door
the weight of
expectation
& for a moment
she is a child
telling the wind
to go home
a girl
punching water
but fists startle
easily, flock,
their murmuration
making the shape
of men pushing
into a room.

//

the men bring the forest
in with them & in their dark
thinkings, animals hunt
themselves & girls in red
hoods turn to thank them
there is something wild

in their civility.
ladies, they say, ladies
their faces red, white
& blue, *ladies*.

//

Jack Catch

Jack Catch rolls back her sleeves
then the skin on her forearms,
cartilage, the muscle, throws a
femur at the men
throws early adolescence
throws a girl at the men
who catch everything
& understand nothing.
she stands her ground
throwing air
handful after handful
until the night blues
& gasps.

//

Dudizile

Dudizile is tired
of stories that end
like this. what is free
is given a high rise,
what is other is given
a new dress,

the gentrification
of fucking.
The men who break
into the bar are men
she has known
all her life. is that a
father over there, an elder
brother? is that the boy
who sat behind her
in school, on the bus,
who walks beside her
each night —
are these the men
who are always behind her?
Dudizile shrugs
picks up her pint
slowly sips
wipes her lips
on her sleeve
whispers to the glass
& sets it free.

//

here we are again

women pushing men

out of their bodies

how many women

does it take

to make a mother.

//

poor men
they had forgotten

that if you
punch a woman

six more grow
from the wound.

//

beyond the bar | a fissure | almost female | flirts with the
vitrine

> *knows that the bonds in glass are their*
> *weakest point*

that when glass breaks it makes the sound of ideas
unravelling, children laughing

Black Triangle

During the Second World War, lesbians in Germany were forced to
wear inverted black triangle badges as a symbol of their *anti-social*
nature. Resistance groups advised them to go undercover, marry
men, wear dresses and give birth.

takes your breath away / this cunnus crossed out / this
boardroom satire / real camp / the vulva excised / sewn
to a sleeve / & called antisocial / one day sooner than
expected / I will sit at a table with Henny Schermann /
smoking / & ask / why didn't you hide? / you could have
climbed in to the body of a woman / & she'll reply /
blowing a smoke mother / but I did / I hid in that body
/ attended to the days / wrote diary entries / but they
saw silhouettes of women / backlit in lavender / slow
dancing / through my shuttered eye lids / my arms
extended beyond their reach / I didn't know where to
hang my breasts / she'll say / blowing a smoke soldier
/ when I applied lipstick / it was a red ring / around a
name / when I let my hair down / everyone climbed up
/ & anyway / they don't tell you / that our enemies dress
as us / it is difficult to tell the difference / between a
skinhead / & a skin head / you know / a brown shirt / was
fashionable for a season / the thing about triangles is /
she'll say / blowing a smoke raven / there are three sides /
your lover, yourself / & whoever is watching.

SCENE ELEVEN

DOWNSTAGE Right. Interior Maryville bar.

LX1: the yellow of teeth, of fingertips.

FX1: a roaring smile. Boystown CD, *You're Just Too Good to be True*.

LX2: follow spot on a chorus line of high kicking butches moving forward in a tidal wave, pushing men back on to the street. The door closes and is bolted. The room erupts into women not moving away from one another. White petals slouch from the ceiling but when they land, they become femme ingenues, each a brunette with a cigarette holder raised to her lips & as the cigarette is lit the smoke that dances from its end becomes a glass bead curtain & through it you are sat, quietly, reading this book.

December

'I ask all who are still at liberty, to take this message seriously
and flee the republic as soon as possible.'

> Final social media post from
> a local LGBT group in
> Chechnya, 2017.

// i

winter. white sun.

a boi dives into a pool
                & does not resurface.

a woman walks through a door
                but does not enter the room.

my name will have been given
                to them by someone I love.

my name a difficult prayer
                my name red confetti

in the wedding of the fist.
                they throw a punch behind them

& I catch it, hear it knock
                bad day to be a girl born outside her
                body.

the knock will come

when the flamingos leave the city.

the knock will come
        when our mothers unbirth us

I will open the door and be stateless.
        my smile a tightrope above an abyss

behind me the closet
        burning.

// ii

the knock is inside us.

// iii

& when I open the door
        everything will fall out.

& what is a closet but the body.
        & what is fire but the lie.

flanked by two men I will walk
        through town in my suit of flames

& everyone we pass will ignite
        the house windows boiling to cataract

the negative strip street curling in the heat
        my fire will call to your fire

& cameras will combust
                a centre fold inferno, typewriter ablaze

newspaper ink curdles
                to uniforms hanging, bright and helpful.

somewhere to the left of here
                a boi revolves, her suit the song of torch
                    something for the people to believe in

// *iv*

the interrogation suite is in the old gay club
                the mirror ball reflects on its mistakes

has each of us imprisoned in its vernacular
                we stare up at one other, sad parenthesis

our beauty refracted into something unwell
                unwelcome in our homes, our bodies

& when the purge walks in
                whistling show tunes, tipping the
                bouncer

others slowly appear
                a rainbow slumped in a gilded cage

a girl still as grass, eyes escape tunnels
                a queen dances in a dress of blue bruises

a brown eyed boi young as love
             swallows her phone and does not cry

a suited woman, asks for a cigarette
        but when it comes, it is a country.

& maybe we will get to write a musical
            something about rainbows and sickles

you will play the lead.
           I won't be here.

It will start when the red curtain pulls apart
            each side no longer speaking to the other

& there we will be, tap dancing in chorus lines
         hollow cheeked and high kicking

barbed wire is a feather boa
         a noose comes in Oxford colours

& when we show our teeth to a lens
          they will be a high wall somewhere

that no one will be able to see behind
           but listen you will say, an ear pressed
           against it

listen

are they not happy? do they not dance?

                    is the melody not a catch?

// v

image #378

a cathedral of girls
            snuffed like candles.

// vi

I will delete every tweet
            but it won't matter

I will be screen shot
            before I am shot

a jury of antelopes
            will wipe their bloody lips

on a photograph of me
            caught in the ropes of a kiss

so little difference between
            a blue bird & a blue bottle

let it saw the day in half:
            a boi reaches for the hand of air

a woman takes her seat at a desk
            each of them a fixed point.

// vii

the first part of me to disappear
        will be my mouth   sugar in water

then my hand, fingers erasing   pencil rubbers
        a shoulder   scent risen to sauna steam

left foot then both legs   torso stripped
        through to the metal seat

delete my heart. evaporate the idea of me.
        a slow striptease down to the breath, the
        belief

the last part of me to disappear
                my absence

// viii

this town is teeming with invisible women.

        they are not there   everywhere.

// ix

because dead names haunt living rooms
because mothers are not photocopiers

because sickles
are for reaping
because girls bend
into corn

because beards seep into black triangles
because triangles grow up to be female

because we
planted a field of
fists
because they fed
us through winter

because nature verses Nietzsche
because the Abyss was a bar

because we were young.
because we were.
because, we.

// x

& now

a reckoning.

the great grief of a generation

a rainbow flag thrown over a coffin.

Eulogy

(i)

& I carry
Roxanne Ellis
within me.
& I carry
Ashanti
Posey within
me.
don't worry
i will raise her
well language
her
on Saturday we
will shop for a
new body
something off
the rack & i
carry Salome
Masooa
within me
Sizakele Sigasa
too (i keep
giving birth to
other people's
children) & I
carry Luana
Barbosa dos
Reis Santos

within me la
camiona &
look there's
Michelle
Abdil too (i
keep giving
birth to the
dead) little
Liyabona
Mabishi is in
there leaning
against
Marielle
Franco who
keeps
unwashing
her face the
heaviest part
of a woman is
her heart the
heaviest part
of us is the
part that is
missing is
everyone else
but I carry
Zoliswa

Nkonyana
within me
& I carry
Simangele
Nhalpo &
Yelena
Grigoryeva
within me
call it blood
song call it
O when you
crack a girl
open the
future spits
out on a neat
slip of paper
enter stage
left: woman as
vending machine
I carry
all of them &
the whole of
the bus, its
passengers &
its route, I
carry the
classroom,

the factory, the
short cut, the
slammed face
of a family all
inside me &
the man she
brushed against
is there too &
the whole of
the white night
the Proud boys
breastfeeding
their nest of
guns I carry the
purge within
me amniotic
pulse over
Chechnya our
pink afterglow
bottled by
the banks
this is where
the rainbow
leads to the
man holding
the other end of
the leash
I'm putting
Uganda inside
me & Russia
& India &
Turkey Iran &
Iraq the whole
of the Middle
East might
as well let the
rest of Africa
in too let's say
the north of
England & the
American
South I'm
going to need
border patrols
they will all be
dead women
asking what you
are carrying.

(ii)

hey. i carry
them all.
every origami
girl folded into
a beast of flight
every avuncular
streetlight
flashing God
each kiss
unravelling into
the outline of a
man asking me
why he cannot
come inside
there is no
more room not
even a hallway
the beds are
piled high with
us arms draped
like drained
rainbows eyes
unlit rooms &

we are in the
walls too & we
are the walls too
& we are the
floor that taught
the foot the joke
running back
into the boy I
dreamed I gave
birth to a wasp
who birthed a
city of wasps
& together
they hunted
their mothers
their stings left
upright in soil
to the hilt map
pins marking
where women
like us used to
drink to rigour
to fall into the

black holes of
dance floors
joey anisha
nonkie nicole
they stabbed
her thirteen
times each
sting a candle
in her cake but
it's okay now
I'm taking her
within me I'm
teaching her
what the water
wants what the
rope knows
how the gun
learned to speak
I'm teaching
her how to hide
behind herself
how to make a
man smile.

SCENE TWELVE

INTERIOR, MARYVILLE daytime.

LX1: the colour of leaving. Outlines sit at uneven tables while another pulls a pint of shadows. As the outlines drink, they fade further. The skeleton of a feather boa flaps once then sleeps. The mouths of the snooker table fall silent.

FX1: the dry bones of music rub against the bar. In the corner the ghost of conversation stands staring at a lit screen, cupped in her palm. Dancers pass through one another, swap bodies & return, their soft pale a static in the soundtrack.

LX2: the overhead lights snap on & the bar shrinks, unthinks itself. & now Maryville is a bar in a snow globe, its ghosts rising and falling, the ground believing the sky.

Butch Proverb No. 3

there is a stained-glass
            window hanging
                        at the back of a place
of worship, *Trade* perhaps,
            or the *Fridge;* let's say
                        it's Friday & the colours
that contrive the design
            are each beautiful but
                        the red is not fond of the
yellow, the way it laughs
            & orange has had enough
                        of green, its sudden.
& no one really believes
            that blue is exactly blue
                        & while they bicker
light loses interest
            & none are aware
                        of the silhouette of the man

approaching   tossing

a   loose stone   between hands.

Trauma: the Opera

and for you, my darling / my high priest of pious
pornography / poetry pimp / you may fuck my Soho-
pink sacred heart / I want to write a book / in which I
live / a story where the girl / gets the girl / & the girl is
herself / a novel where I return / to find a six year old
child opening a bedroom door/ and I shotgun / *don't
do that* / stop all that opera / there is still so much to
learn / but how do I write / that if *war is God's way of
teaching Americans geography* / then maybe this / o-god
/ oubliette / is God's way of teaching woman history /
how do I ask her to lift skin / organise dust / pin back
the night / excavate, glue / I know / that if you press your
ear against my shell / you will hear Bangkok / my Koh
San Road / or the itch of Moss Side pavements / the
call of corner boys / slouching with bees in their mouths
/ tonight / you will hear reindeer over Rotherham,
children / my mother's funeral laugh / you will hear
black women / teaching / scratching chalk outlines on
blackboard skin / my shell sings the sirens of Mount
Sinjara / my song seduces war / listen / can you hear a
child ticking / the slow-dance of bones beside Phnom
Penn brothels / my dropped vase / kintsugi cunt / paint
all the scars in Poundshop glitter, girl / are all women
/ inside other women / & how do I write / that you are
there too / pretty dust girl / curled deep in your cave of
remarkable horror / inside yourself / uroboros / smiling
a no / putting your headphones on / staring into your
hands / unscrewing your fists / every time you / open
your mouth / a white man jumps out / & wolfs you / how
do I write that / there is a grave at the grave meeting of
my legs / & no one goes there after dark / except with

nets / to catch all these beautiful ghosts / pinning them to novels / pages plucked / vajazzled / & while we are at it / how should I write that / I had all your ghost babies / they live together at the edge of the woods / & don't write home anymore.

thank you for listening. lay a wreath where the two roads pleat. photocopy my photograph. return to me once a year. tell them a story.

make me live.

Watch Joelle
perform 'C+nto'

Watch Joelle
perform 'Trauma:
The Opera'

ACKNOWLEDGEMENTS

This work has been made possible by a grant from Arts Council England.

My first thanks are to Lisa Mead, who commissioned this work on behalf of Apples & Snakes to include in their thirty-five-year celebration event, *Rallying Cry*. The world of *C+nto* was created by director Rob Watt and stage designed by Bethany Wells, and it is their world that helped me find my own again. Thank you. Thanks also to the Battersea Arts Centre where *C+nto* premiered, and to BBC Contains Strong Language Festival. Thanks to Paul Burston and Polari Literary Salon for allowing me to record live from Heaven, and for the legacy you have gifted the LGBT community.

Huge thanks to Lynn Gaspard at The Westbourne Press for the belief and support, and to my agent Laura MacDougall of United Agents for pushing on my behalf.

Thanks to my producer and international events agent, Tom MacAndrew, who makes the impossible believable. Thanks also to Writers Republic in Australia and Tim Loydell for the continued support of my work. Thank you Faith Lawrence who had the idea for the BBC Radio 4 programme *Butch*, and who continues to produce inspiring and necessary work.

Thank you Inua Ellams for agreeing to help guide this book onto the page and on into a theatre show. Your insight, support and acumen have been invaluable. Equally, thank you Jay Bernard for your friendship and kindness in helping me tighten the text. I look forward to our next fictional dinner.

Without the work of LGBT archives such as the Lesbian and Gay Archives housed at the Bishopsgate Institute, this book would not have been possible. It is a house of remembrance and I hope I have honoured you. Thanks also to KENRIC for the constant support and interviews.

Thanks seem hollow when offered to my good friend Anthony Anaxagorou for the lengthy conversations, poetry forensics and extravagance of thinking that sustain me.

Thanks to the contemporary poets, authors and friends who inspire me and who have given the kind of encouragement that leads to writing a book — Salena Godden, Zena Edwards, Raymond Antrobus, Fran Lock, Sabrina Mahfouz, Adam Kammerling, Lisa Luxx, Courttia Newland and Val McDermid, to name a few.

Collectivity is the antidote to cultural fascism and I am enlivened and challenged every day by the team behind Out-Spoken. If you want to develop as an artist, surround yourself with people you respect. Thank you Karim Kamar, Sam Junior Bromfield and Patricia Ferguson for always raising the bar.

Thanks to the dykes, bois and butches who inspired this work, which is essentially a love letter to you all. So, thank you Rebel Dykes, thank you club comrades, chill out crew, the regulars in the Royal Oak or Artful Dodger or The Welly in the '90s. Thank you to some of the most courageous humans I have met and loved. Thanks to my bois Kim Allmark, Nickie Counsell, Michelle Pollock and Sophie Mitchell.

Finally, the greatest gratitude to Marie Seary who has listened to every story, character breakdown, idea of a poem that made its way into this collection, and a whole lot more that didn't. This is who we are.

www.joelletaylor.co.uk
@jtaylortrash

CREDITS

Some of poems in this collection have appeared in earlier versions in books or have been commissioned. I am grateful to the following platforms and anthologies for including this work.

C+nto — commissioned for *Rallying Cry*, Apples & Snakes, Battersea Arts Centre 2018, 2019 / BBC Contains Strong Language Festival (2020).

Sections of *C+nto* have also appeared on *QueerStories* Podcast (2019) and *Butch* BBC Radio 4 (2020), produced by Faith Lawrence.

The Unbelong — commissioned for *RAP Party* (2019), produced by Inua Ellams and Theresa Lola.

Trauma: The Opera — *Witches, Warriors & Workers*, edited by Fran Lock & Jane Burn (Culture Matters 2020)

Homosapien — *Pogo Serotonin*, edited by Stephen Watt (the Buzzcocks 2020)

December — commissioned as a part of Writers Bloc, a Writing on the Wall residency.

This book was written to a playlist of '90s music popular in the gay bars of that time. The playlist can be found at www.joelletaylor.co.uk